Questions and Answers: Countries

Ireland

A Question and Answer Book

by Mary Dodson Wade

Consultant:
Padraig O'Cearuill
Glucksman Ireland House
New York University

Capstone
press®
Mankato, Minnesota

Fact Finders is published by Capstone Press
151 Good Counsel Drive, P.O. Box 669, Mankato, Minnesota 56002.
www.capstonepress.com

Library of Congress Cataloging-in-Publication Data
Wade, Mary Dodson.
    Ireland : a question and answer book / by Mary Dodson Wade.
    p. cm. —(Questions and answers—countries)
    Summary: "Describes the geography, history, economy, and culture of Ireland in a
question-and-answer format"—Provided by publisher.
    Includes bibliographical references and index.
    ISBN–13: 978–0–7368–6410–7 (hardcover)
    ISBN–10: 0–7368–6410–5 (hardcover)
    1. Ireland—Miscellanea—Juvenile literature. I. Title. II. Series: Fact finders.
Questions and answers. Countries.
DA906.W322 2007
949.12—dc22   2006005056

Editorial Credits
Silver Editions, editorial, design, and production; Kia Adams, set designer; Ortelius Design,
    Inc., cartographer; Jo Miller, photo researcher; Scott Thoms, photo editor

Photo Credits
Art Directors/B R Woods, 4; Capstone Press Archives, 29 (bill); Corbis/Anne W. Krause,
18; Corbis/Dave Bartruff, 25; Corbis/Gideon Mendel, 17; Corbis/Jack Fields, 27; Corbis/
Stapleton Collection, 20; Corbis/Tim Thompson, 13; Corbis/William Manning, cover
(background); Getty Images Inc./AFP/Javier Soriano, 9; Getty Images Inc./Patrick Riviere,
8; Getty Images Inc./Stone/Mark Joseph, 1; Index Stock Imagery/Jacque Denzer Parker,
cover (foreground); Index Stock Imagery/Timothy O'Keefe, 16; Photo Courtesy of Paul
Baker, 29 (coins); Richard T. Nowitz, 7; Shutterstock/Amra Pasic, 23; Shutterstock/Andriy
Doriy, 24; Shutterstock/Dimitrious Kaisaris, 29 (flag); Shutterstock/Eoghan McNally, 19;
Stockbyte, 11, 12; SuperStock/age fotostock, 6; SuperStock/Steve Vidler, 15, 21

Table of Contents

Features

Where is Ireland?

Ireland is a country on an island west of Great Britain, in the North Atlantic Ocean. It is about the size of the U.S. state of West Virginia.

Ireland's land is both rugged and flat. Steep hills and mountains cover Ireland's coastline. Low plains blanket the center of the country. The Shannon River divides these plains from north to south.

The Burren lies along the western coast of Ireland.

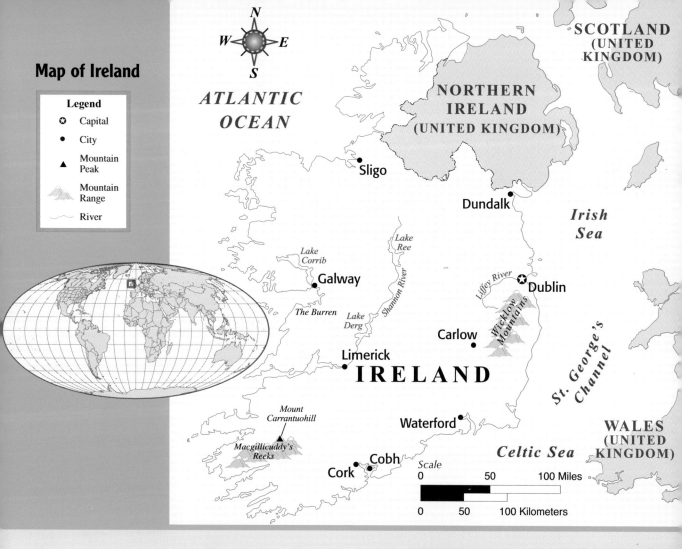

Map of Ireland

Legend

- ✪ Capital
- ● City
- ▲ Mountain Peak
- Mountain Range
- River

ATLANTIC OCEAN

SCOTLAND (UNITED KINGDOM)

NORTHERN IRELAND (UNITED KINGDOM)

● Sligo

● Dundalk

Irish Sea

Lake Ree

Lake Corrib

● Galway

Shannon River

Liffey River

✪ ● Dublin

Wicklow Mountains

The Burren

Lake Derg

● Carlow

● Limerick

IRELAND

Mount Carrantuohill

Macgillicuddy's Reeks

● Waterford

St. George's Channel

WALES (UNITED KINGDOM)

● Cobh

Cork ●

Celtic Sea

Scale

0   50   100 Miles

0   50   100 Kilometers

Rain falls about 150 to 225 days a year in Ireland. The rain turns the plains so green that Ireland is known as the Emerald Isle.

One place that is not green is the Burren, which means rocky place. The ground is limestone rock. Wildflowers and grasses grow up through the cracks in the rocks.

5

When did Ireland become a country?

Ireland became a separate country from the United Kingdom in 1921. The United Kingdom had ruled Ireland for 500 years. Before that, Ireland was home to many **clans**. The clans often fought each other. One clan leader invited the English to help him defeat another clan. Eventually, the English took control of Ireland and it became part of the United Kingdom.

Fact!

Ireland has many ancient stone forts, underground burial places, and mounds with carved symbols. Little is known about who created them.

This statue of Charles Stewart Parnell stands in the center of Dublin. Parnell fought for Ireland's independence from the United Kingdom.

For many years, the Irish fought for freedom. Finally in 1921, the Assembly of Ireland signed a treaty with the United Kingdom. Under the treaty, most of Ireland became a free country. A small northern part of the island, however, remained part of the United Kingdom.

What type of government does Ireland have?

Ireland is a **republic**. Irish people vote for their leaders. All Irish citizens can vote when they become 18 years of age.

The president of Ireland is elected every seven years. Presidents can serve only two terms. One of the president's main jobs is to represent Ireland at events.

Fact!

In 1990, Ireland elected its first female president. Mary Robinson served as president for seven years.

In 1997, Mary McAleese became the eighth president of Ireland.

Ireland's **Taoiseach**, or Prime Minister, runs the government. The Taoiseach is nominated by the House of Representatives and is appointed by the president. The House of Representatives makes the country's laws. It meets in Dublin, the capital city.

What kind of housing does Ireland have?

Until 50 years ago, most Irish people lived and worked on farms. Farm families usually lived in stone houses with **thatched** roofs. Narrow roads led through small villages. Cars shared the road with sheep and cattle. But in the last 20 years, Ireland has seen big changes.

Where do people in Ireland live?

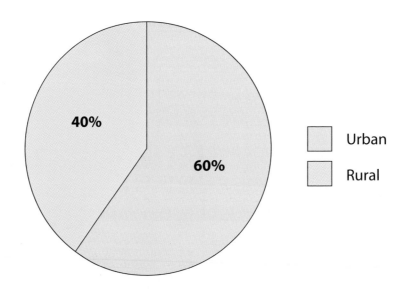

40%

60%

☐ Urban

☐ Rural

Houses with thatched roofs can still been seen in small Irish villages today.

Today, most Irish people no longer work on farms. About half of Ireland's population lives within 60 miles (97 kilometers) of Dublin. Traditional housing has given way to modern houses and apartments.

What are Ireland's forms of transportation?

Because it is an island, people and goods travel to and from Ireland by air and sea. There are five main seaports and three major airports.

Within Ireland, there are other forms of transportation. Ships travel the Shannon River. Rail lines link cities all over the country.

Fact!

Cobh is a seaport in County Cork on the south coast. The Titanic made a final stop in Cobh, formerly Queenstown, before setting out on its fatal voyage in 1912.

Ferries take people to and from the many islands that surround Ireland's mainland.

Many people in Ireland travel by car or bus. Roads link Dublin with all the other major cities of Ireland.

In the days before cars, everybody walked. Hikers still take holidays to explore the mountains and ancient places that dot the Irish countryside.

13

What are Ireland's major industries?

Over the last 50 years, industry has replaced agriculture as the main employer in Ireland. Today, the country is a leading producer of zinc ores and has one of the world's largest zinc and lead mines. Factories produce steel to build ships and automobiles.

About 7 percent of Irish workers still farm. Potatoes, wheat, sugar beets, and barley are all grown in Ireland. Some farmers raise cattle and sheep.

What does Ireland import and export?	
Imports	**Exports**
chemicals	chemicals
clothing	computers
machinery	machinery
petroleum	equipment
petroleum products	pharmaceuticals

THERE IS NO CHARGE FOR
KISSING THE BLARNEY STONE.
REMOVE ALL LOOSE VALUABLES
BEFORE DOING SO.

The Blarney Stone is hard to reach. People have to lie on their backs in order to kiss it.

Tourism is also a major industry. People come to see Ireland's many castles. Near the city of Cork, people visit Blarney Castle. They kiss the Blarney Stone to get the gift of expressive speech. Tourists also take home Ireland's famous Waterford crystal.

What is school like in Ireland?

Irish children must start primary school by age 6. Primary schools are free. Parents can choose any school as long as it has room. The government pays the cost of schools, though most are run by religious organizations.

Secondary school is for children ages 12 to 18. Students must attend school until they are 16. Most secondary schools are free, but families must pay for books and uniforms.

Fact!

All schools teach Gaelic, the first official language of Ireland.

Schoolchildren pray during class at St. Brigid's Girls School in Dublin.

The school year in Ireland begins in September. Holidays come at Christmas, Easter, and mid-term breaks. School is out during July and August.

What are Ireland's favorite sports and games?

Traditional sports in Ireland are Gaelic football and hurling. In football, teams of 15 players kick a soccer-like ball toward a goal. In hurling, players must get a ball past a goal using long hockey-like sticks.

The Irish also enjoy playing soccer and rugby. Irish people are very loyal to the professional teams in these sports.

Fact!

The earliest written record of handball in Ireland is in the town of Galway in 1527. The order said people could not play on the walls of the town.

Two Irish teams play in the Leinster football championship in Dublin.

Horseracing has been a sport in Ireland for hundreds of years. Steeplechase racing started when two men decided to race from one church to another. In this kind of race, horses jump ditches and fences.

What are the traditional art forms in Ireland?

Music is a big part of Irish tradition. The ancient symbol of Ireland is the **harp**. Today, musicians entertain at pubs and small gatherings. They play fiddles, tin whistles, guitars, and goatskin drums called *bodhráns*.

Irish step dancing is a traditional dance form. Some common step dances are jigs and reels. In a step dance, the legs and feet move very fast. The upper body stays still.

Fact!

The Book of Kells is often called the most beautiful book in the world. About 1,200 years ago, Irish monks filled each page with bright colors and designs. The book's cover was made of gold and jewels.

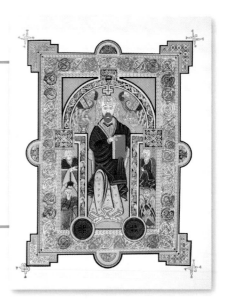

Each school of dance has its own colorful costume.

Storytelling is also an art form in Ireland. Irish people fill their conversations with stories about people and events. There are also professional storytellers called *seanachaidhe*. They can repeat hundreds of ancient stories without changing a word.

What holidays do the Irish celebrate?

The Irish celebrate many Roman Catholic holidays. Christmas and Easter are important family holidays. The Christmas season in Ireland lasts until January 6. The three days before Easter, known as the Triduum, is a very **solemn** holiday in Ireland. People **fast** and go to church. On Easter Sunday, some people celebrate with a dance contest called a *Pruthog*. The prize is a cake that the winner shares with everyone.

What other holidays do people in Ireland celebrate?

May Day
New Year's Day
St. Stephen's Day

The best known Irish holiday is on March 17, St. Patrick's Day. St. Patrick is Ireland's **patron saint**. People around the world wear **shamrocks** and the color green to celebrate. In Ireland, there are many festivals with music and dancing.

What are the traditional foods of Ireland?

Irish cooks fix hearty foods. They serve crusty brown soda bread made from wheat flour. A full Irish breakfast includes sausage, bacon, eggs, Irish pudding, baked beans, broiled tomato, bread, butter, and tea.

Fact!

A fungus ruined the potato crops in Ireland 150 years ago. Potatoes were the main food of farm families. Thousands of people starved, while many others left the country in search of a better life.

Most hotels and inns in Ireland serve traditional Irish breakfasts.

Potatoes have always been a large part of the Irish diet. *Boxty* is a baked dish of potatoes mashed with butter, buttermilk, and flour. *Champ* is boiled potatoes mashed with butter, milk, and scallions.

What is family life like in Ireland?

Irish families are often large. Children usually live with parents until they marry. Elderly relatives remain with the family.

In the past, women stayed at home to run the house and raise the children. Today, many women take jobs outside the home.

What are the ethnic backgrounds of people in Ireland?

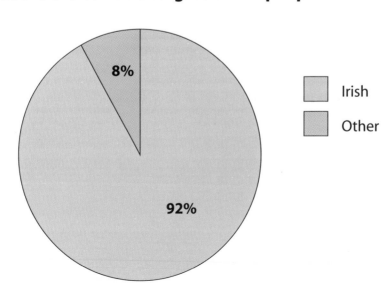

8%

92%

Irish

Other

A priest leads a choir during a First Communion family celebration.

Families are close in Ireland. Many Irish stories and songs celebrate people who have done heroic acts for their family. Families gladly welcome people into their homes. Since ancient times, it has been considered rude to turn away strangers.

Ireland Fast Facts

Official name:

Ireland
Éire, Gaelic for Ireland
Sometimes called
*   Republic of Ireland*

Land area:

26,599 square miles
(69,890 square kilometers)

Average annual precipitation (Dublin):

29.2 inches (74 centimeters)

Average January temperature (Dublin):

41 degrees Fahrenheit
(5 degrees Celsius)

Average July temperature (Dublin):

59 degrees Fahrenheit
(15 degrees Celsius)

Population:

4,015,676 people

Capital city:

Dublin

Languages:

Gaelic and English

Natural resources:

Peat, copper, lead, zinc, silver, gypsum, limestone

Religions:

Roman Catholic	*88.4%*
Church of Ireland	*3%*
Other Christian	*1.6%*
Other	*3.5%*
None	*3.5%*

Money and Flag

Money:

Ireland's money is the euro. In 2006, one euro equaled $1.20 U.S. dollars. One euro equaled 1.4 Canadian dollars.

Flag:

Ireland's flag has three vertical bars: green, white, and orange. The green stands for Ireland's Catholics, the orange for Protestants, and the white for peace between the two.

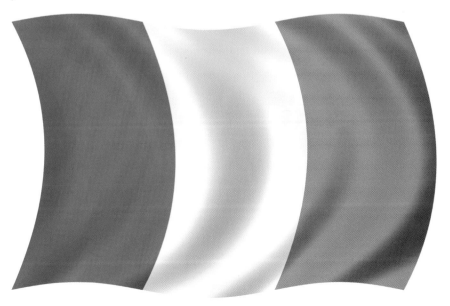

Learn to Speak Gaelic

Gaelic is Ireland's first official language. Learn to speak some Gaelic words using the chart below.

English	Gaelic	Pronunciation
hello	Dia dhuit	(JEE-ah GHOOCH)
good-bye	Slán agat	(SLAWN UG-ut)
How are you?	Conas ata tu?	(CUNN-us UTHAW TOO)
thank you	Go raibh maith agat	(GUH ROH MOH UG-ut)
welcome	Fáilte	(FAHLT-shuh)

Glossary

clan (KLAN)—a large family group

fast (FAST)—to give up eating food for a period of time

harp (HARP)—a large musical instrument with strings that you play by plucking

patron saint (PAY-trun SAYNT)—a saint in the Catholic church to whom a person or place is dedicated

republic (ree-PUHB-lik)—a government in which officials are elected by the people

shamrock (SHAM-rok)—a small, green plant with three leaves

solemn (SOL-uhm)—very serious

Taoiseach (TEESHAH)—the leader of Ireland's parliament, a government body that makes laws

thatch (THATCH)—a roof made of straw, leaves, or grasses

tourism (TOOR-iz-um)—the business of providing entertainment, food, and lodging for travelers

Internet Sites

FactHound offers a safe, fun way to find Internet sites related to this book. All of the sites on FactHound have been researched by our staff.

Here's how:
1. Visit *www.facthound.com*
2. Choose your grade level.
3. Type in this book ID **0736864105** for age-appropriate sites. You may also browse subjects by clicking on letters, or by clicking on pictures and words.
4. Click on the **Fetch It** button.

FactHound will fetch the best sites for you!

Read More

Daley, Patrick. *Ireland.* Steadwell Books World Tour. Austin, Texas: Raintree Steck-Vaughn, 2002.

Fontes, Justine, and Ron Fontes. *Ireland. A to Z.* New York: Children's Press, 2003.

Krull, Kathleen. *A Pot O' Gold: A Treasury of Irish Stories, Poetry, Folklore, and (Of Course) Blarney.* New York: Hyperion, 2004.

Index